LONDON
CITY CHURCHES

By Colin Pitt

ISBN 978-1-7398450-7-0

CP PRESS

CONTENTS

All Saints, Ennismore Gardens was built 1846 - 1849 by L. Vulliamy but the front was built in 1892 by C. H. Townsend.

All Saints, is decorated in Arts and Crafts Sgrafitto by Heywood Sumner. It is now the Dormation of the Mother of God and All Saints of the Russian Orthodox Church.

The contract for All Saints, Margaret Street was signed on 1st September 1850 and went to John Kelk a West End builder based in Margaret Street.

All Saints Day 1852 had been the date aimed at for consecration but the church stayed shut for several years after this with differences over how to finish the interior being the main reason for delays. The church was finally consecrated in May 1859 with estimated expenditure in the region of £70,000 and The Prince Consort was among early visitors to All Saints.

The church's plan consisted of a three-bay nave that was about double the width of the flanking aisles, and a two-bay chancel. The westernmost bay of the nave on the South side supports the tower, above the nave arches a cornice supports the clorestory. Triplets of windows over the arches alternate with wider blanks over the piers.

The colour and patterns visible in All Saints date from the original finishes of 1852, the decoration of the later 1850's, Butterfield's additions and alterations between the 1870's and 1890's, Comper's alterations after 1909 and restoration by Colin Kerr since 2007.

All Saints was built 1849 - 1859 to the designs of architect William Butterfield.

The alterpiece is by William Dyce.

The highly decorated interior was an inspiration for artists and architects of the Arts and Crafts movement.

William Butterfield was also the architect of St. Augustine, Queens Gate.

The church's circular portico acts as a pivot and its rectangular nave is rotated on a north-east axis. All Souls was built 1822-1824 by architect John Nash.

Summerson observed, "It is nevertheless a curiously ambiguous design... both modern French and old English."

The Church of Holy Redeemer at 24 Exmouth Market, Angel was built in 1887 by J. D. Sedding.

In giant gilt letters 'Christo Liberator" stands above the entrance.

London's Arts and Crafts church by J. D. Sedding, built 1888 - 1890.

The stained glass of the east windows was made by Morris and Company to the designs of Burne-Jones.

St. Anselm and St. Cecilia Church is at 70 Lincoln's Inn Fields.

The church was built around 1909 to the designs of Frederick Walters to replace the Sardinian Embassy Chapel that was demolished to make way for Kingsway.

In 1853 the Chapel was called after it's titular saint, Anselm and in 1861 the Pastor Father William O' Connor added St. Cecilia as the second patron.

St. Anselm and St. Cecilia church has been a Grade II listed building since 1974.

St Augustine's was built 1870 - 1877 by John Pearson.

St. Augustine's is sometimes called the Cathedral of North London on account of its grandeur. The tower is seventy-seven metres high.

St. Clement Danes was built 1680 by Wren but the tower by Gibbs was added 1719 - 1720.

St. Clement is the Patron Saint of Mariners.

Below can be seen the staircase of St. Clement Danes.

St. Clement Danes was bombed in the Second World War and was rebuilt as a memorial to the Royal Air Force.

The main body of the Church of St. Francis of Assisi, Pottery Lane, was built by Jackson and Shaw in 1859-1860 to the designs of Henry Clutton. The building work was supervised by John Francis Bentley and the church opened on 2nd February 1860.

Bentley designed additions including the presbytery and school which were completed by 1863. The school and presbytery are in the same thirteenth-century French Gothic style as the church.

St. George, Hanover Square was built 1721 - 1724 by John James.

The portico is Corinthian and the north and south elevations each have five bays. Inside are galleries on piers, topped with Corinthian columns supporting the vaulted ceiling.

St Ignatius occupies a corner site with frontages on Stamford Hill and St. Ann's Road. The architects were Benedict and J. H. Beart Foss.

St. Ignatius is ministered by the Society of Jesus who founded it on 1894. The Jesuits decided to dedicate the church to their order's founder, St. Ignatius of Loyola.

The principal dimensions of St. Ignatius Church are a Nave of 105 feet by 32 feet and 53 feet high, a Sanctuary of 37 feet by 32 feet and Towers of 14 feet 9 inches by 14 feet 9 inches and 119 feet high to the ridge of the roof.

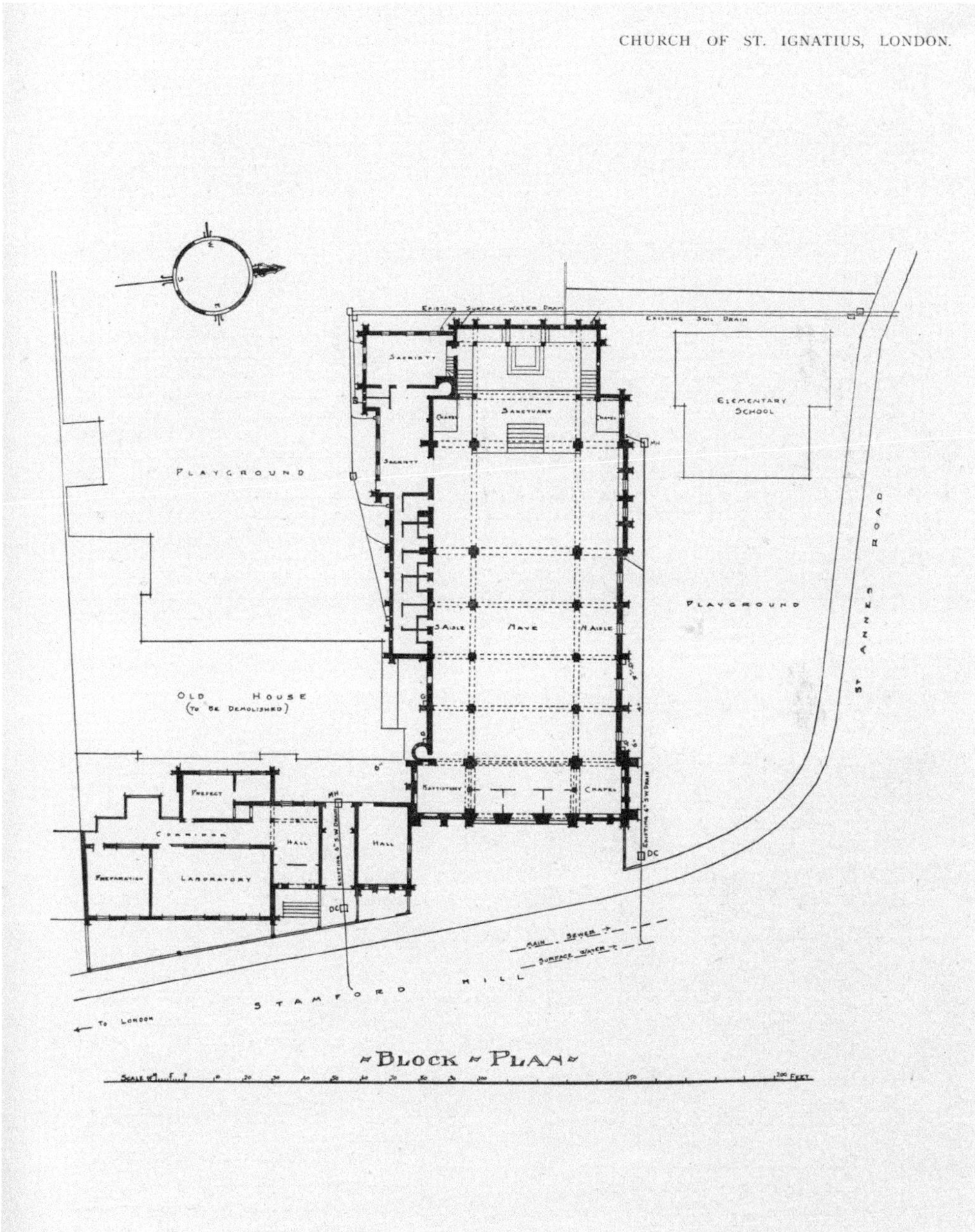

The exterior of St. Ignatius Church is faced with two-inch Belgian bricks with Kentish Rag and reconstructed-stone dressings. Green Westmoreland slates cover the roof. Glazing and headed Glass Work were by William Morris & Co. Ltd.

St. James, Piccadilly was built 1676 - 1684 by Christopher Wren but Albert Richardson added the copper spire. Wren thought a congregation of two thousand people could be accomodated.

The virtuoso alterpiece carvings are by Grinling Gibbons.

St. John was built 1744 - 1747. The interior was altered in 1872 by S. P. Cockerell and Ionic columns support arches which cut into the tunnel vault.

Those buried here include George du Maurier, John Constable and Richard Norman Shaw.

St. John, Waterloo Road, Waterloo was built 1822 - 1824 by F. O. Bedford.

It is one of the many 'Waterloo churches' built by the Church Commissioners.

St. John's Wood Chapel was built in 1813 by Thomas Hardwick.

Inside Tuscan columns support glazed galleries.

The original site of the Royal College of St. Katherine had been next to the Tower of London.

In 1825 the hospital was rebuilt in Regent's Park. It was designed by Ambrose Poynter.

St. Martin-in-the-fields was built 1721 - 1726 by James Gibbs. There was a redevelopment by Eric Parry Associates (2006 - 2008) and you now see a freestanding glass entrance kiosk in the passage north of the church.

To the east end there is a large Venetian window with newly created glass by Shirazeh Housiary. The interior has galleries on three sides with a vault over the nave on Corinthian columns.

St. Mary Woolnoth was built 1716 - 1727 by Nicholas Hawksmoor and occupies a site on Lombard Street and King William Street. The 'Tower' is so broad that it occupies almost the full width of the West front

The interior is square with an inner square defined by twelve Corinthian columns bunched into the corners.

There were alterations to the interior in 1875 - 1876 by Butterfield resulting in galleries previously occupying the north and south sides being dismantled.

At one time one of the entrances to Bank Underground Station was in the crypt of St. Mary Woolnoth church. It can be seen here but is no longer used. Bank Station's ticket hall had been constructed underneath the church.

In choosing a parishoner as architect, the Vestry selected Thomas Hardwick of Berners Street. With St. John's Wood Chapel well advanced Hardwick was appointed to design the New Road chapel in April 1813. Thomas Hardwick's design went out to tender in June 1813 and the lowest bidder was Richard Wade. By June 1814 the Vestry decided Hardwick should aggrandize the chapel into a church. The final cost in 1817 was estimated at around £62,000. Sculptor Henry Westmacott was commissioned to model the capitals for the columns and pilasters. Consecration, originally scheduled for 31 December, took place on 4 February 1817. The public face of St. Mary towards Marylebone Road with an approach from the north was acquired when Nash's York Gate was laid out.

Above the church and garden can be seen from the south-east.

The interior originally had two levels of galleries on three sides supported by slender iron columns. The upper galleries on the north and south sides were removed in the late nineteenth century by Thomas Harris.

Superb interior of St. Mary, Marylebone Road.

St. Mary-le-Strand was built 1714 - 1717 by James Gibbs. Gibbs was Hawksmoor's contemporary. The church is now stranded on a large traffic island. The inside has neither aisles nor galleries but is a simple box with a coffered segmental vault.

At 68 metres, St. Mary-le-Bow is second only to St. Bride in height.

St. Mary-le-Bow was built 1670 - 1683 by Christopher Wren.

St. Mary's symmetrical west front has a centre tower of London stock brick.

The church was built 1824 - 1827 by W. and H. W. Inwood.

St. Mary, Wyndham Place, was built in 1823 by Robert Smirke.

Smirke's use of the Greek Revival Style is seen with the gallery and the doric columns supporting the curved coffered ceiling.

St. Michael and All Angels was built 1879 - 1880 by Richard Norman Shaw as was the Tabard Inn and Stores just opposite.

The four-bay nave is in red brick with small perpendicular and rectagonal stone windows.

The tiled roof has a white timber railing to the eaves.

Maurice Adams added the Parish Hall and north aisle in 1887.

St. Paul, Covent Garden was built 1631 - 1638 by Inigo Jones.

The main door to the church is through Inigo Place off Bedford Street. This is the other side of the church.

In 1795 a fire destroyed the interior and the restoration by Thomas Hardwick failed to replace the side galleries.

The Earl of Bedford instructed Inigo Jones saying he only wanted a church like a barn. Inigo Jones said that he would build the 'handsomest barn in England.' The church is also known as the actor's church.

St. Paul is a Grade II listed Anglican church built in 1843 by Thomas Cundy.

The building was consecrated in 1843 and the chancel with its rood screen and striking reredos was added in 1892 by G. F. Bodley.

St. Peters Church was built 1824 - 1827 by architect Henry Hakewill.

St. Peters Church is a neoclassical building with a hexastyle portico with Ionic columns and a clock tower. It was rebuilt after fires in 1837 and 1991. The chancel and transepts were added by Arthur Blomfield in 1875.

The Oxford Chapel, known since 1832 as St. Peter's Vere Street, was built 1721 - 1724 for the inhabitants of houses around Cavendish Square. The building is no longer a chapel but the home of the London Institute for Contemporary Christianity. It is the sole survivor in its original form of Marylebone's 18th - century proprietary chapels.

The Oxford Chapel was paid for by Lord Harley and designed by James Gibbs. Gibbs was also responsible for St. Mary le Strand (1714 - 1717) and Gibbs had also extended the Harley's house at Wimpole, Cambridgeshire.

The chapel is essentially a rectangular grey-brick box that incorporates a western ante-chapel, with galleries on three sides reached by stairs either side of the ante-chapel. Arcades of giant Corinthian columns on high pedestals carry the galleries. The ceiling of the main vault has Artari and Bagutti's Italian rococo plasterwork. It was here that in 1734 that the Earl of Oxford's daughter, Lady Margeret Harley, married the 2nd Duke of Portland. In 1817 the Crown bought the Oxford Chapel and other proprietary chapels in the area from the 4th Duke of Portland.

In 1982 - 1983 the church was adapted for the London Institute for Contemporary Christianity. Timber and glass partitions were inserted under the galleries to make offices and reading rooms. The galleries on the north side were converted into a library.

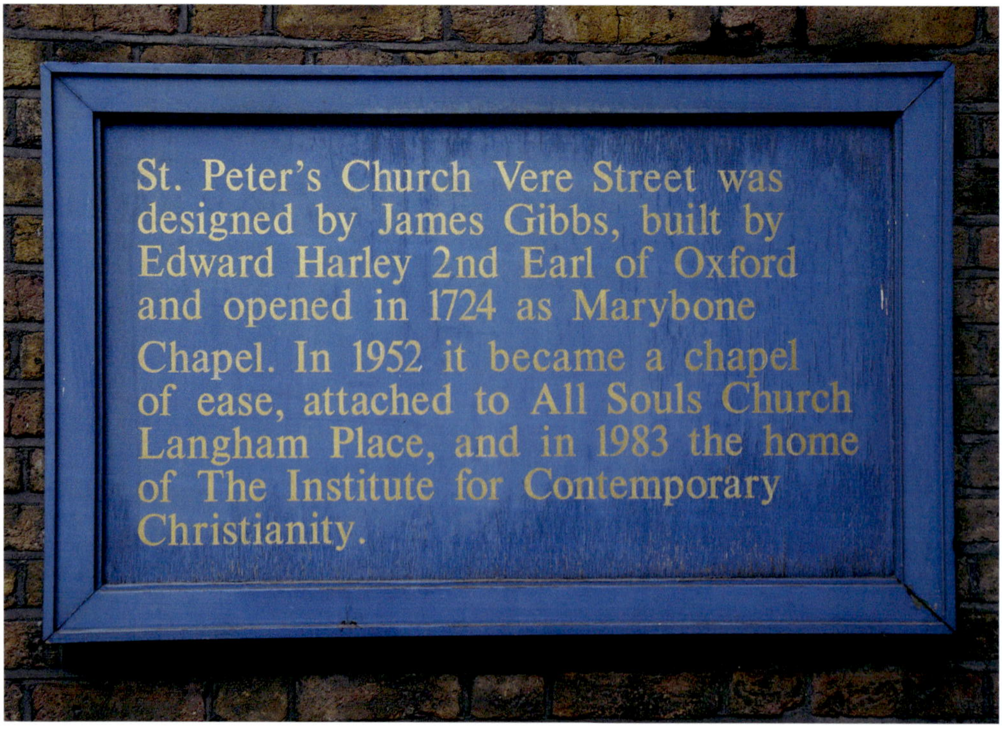

Theologian F. D. Maurice succeeded the Rev. Edward Scobell and preached here from 1860 until 1869.

St. Peters Vere Street, has a stained glass window designed by Edward Burne-Jones.

St. Peters Vere Street became a daughter church of All Souls, Langham Place, for which it stood in during post-war rebuilding there.

St. Peters Italian Catholic Church is a basilica-style church that was consecrated 16 April 1863 and built by the architect Sir John Miller-Bryson. The frontal section of the church consists of a loggia and portico with twin arches, above which are three alcoves.

St. Peters Italian Catholic Church is modelled on the Basilica San Crisogono in Rome.

The church was built at the request of Saint Vincent Pallotti and remains under the control of the Pallotine order which he founded.

The church was intended for the growing number of Italian immigrants in London in the mid 19th century.

St. Patrick's was built 1891 - 1893 by Kelly and Birchall.

St Patrick's is one of several churches in Soho to have served various generations of settlers.

The elevation to Sutton Row is in fine red brickwork.

The Ukrainian Catholic Cathedral ex King's Weigh House Chapel was built 1889 - 1891 by Alfred Waterhouse. The Duke Street facade is asymmetrical with a tall tower on the south-west corner.

St. Vedast-alias-Foster was built 1670-1673 in Foster Lane by Christopher Wren. There is a post-war rectory by Dykes Bowyer created in 1960.

The interior is a plain flat-ceilinged box.

St. Vedast-alias-Foster has Portland stone facades with round headed windows.

The spire of St. Vedast-alias-Foster was added later (1709-1712). Interior is plain with a flat ceiling and a Tuscan arcade to a single aisle south of the nave.

The Church of the Immaculate Conception, Farm Street, was built 1844-1849 by J. J. Scoles. The high altar was by Augustus Welby Pugin.

There are entrances from both Farm Street and Mount Street Gardens to the church. The nave and aisles are of eight bays.

Westminster Cathedral, Archbishop's House and Clergy House were built 1895 - 1903 by John Francis Bentley.

John Francis Bentley was asked by Cardinal Vaughan to build Westminster Cathedral in Byzantine style possibly to avoid stylistic competition with Westminster Abbey.

The church has a great nave roofed with three shallow concrete coppered domes. The nave is flanked with narrow aisles with galleries above.

The side chapels are finished with much mosaic above the marble.

The Stations of the Cross are the most important artwork in the Cathedral and were carved by Eric Gill between 1913 and 1918.